D1366280

Unrelenting Grace

A United Methodist Way of Life

Kenneth H. Carter Jr.

Abingdon Press

UNRELENTING GRACE:
A UNITED METHODIST WAY OF LIFE

Library of Congress Control Number: 2023933660
ISBN: 978-1-7910-3069-8

Contents

Contents

Introduction

United Methodists were an established and somewhat stable church, but all of that is changing. We could list a few of the reasons: pandemic, polarization, disaffiliation, and exhaustion. Yet as unsettling as this disruption has become, we have a more foundational promise: God is with us and for us.

When our church buildings are dwelling places for God, which they are consecrated to be, we will make space for an unrelenting grace that stretches us, mystifies us, unravels us, and ultimately heals us. The Old Testament covenant (Ezekiel 37) and its New Testament echo (John 1) inevitably take us beyond ourselves; this was Paul's disruption (Acts 9), Peter's dream (Acts 10), and the early church's decision (Acts 15). God's dwelling place always points back to an ancient promise—"I will bless those who bless you, . . . all the families of the earth will be blessed because

1

of you" (Genesis 12:3)—which carries us into the future promise—"Go and make disciples of all nations. . . . I myself will be with you every day" (Matthew 28:20).

God's dwelling place is with *us*. We need to trust again in the nearness of divine presence. After a pandemic, many of our church buildings look and feel different. Because of disaffiliation, many have a different relationship to these spaces.

We are learning again that God's dwelling place is with us. We know it is of God if we are becoming more loving (1 John 4); and we know the love is of God if we love (and not merely tolerate) those outside our communities (Luke 10), those who are sinners (Romans 5), and those who we perceive to be our enemies (Matthew 5). The cross of Jesus is the outward and visible sign of this love. It is such a powerful sign that we place it prominently at the center of many of our church buildings, and even in our homes.

The love of God "puts up with all things, trusts in all things, hopes for all things, endures all things" (1 Corinthians 13:7). Love is not a sentiment; it is a sacrifice. Love means staying at the table (John 13) with disciples who are imperfect and ambitious. Love is the patience (Galatians 5) to allow God to remove our defects. This is *purgation*. It is easier to separate from the imperfection we see in the other person than to do the spiritual work of confessing our own sin (Isaiah 6).

And yet here, in our confession, God is with us. The temple of God's presence can be wherever we are. We will know it is of God if it changes us, if it forces us to reconsider the way we have judged others and wanted to live apart from them, if we have to give up something we cherish. We will know it is of God if we find ourselves making space for something greater that God wants to give us.

This gift is the unrelenting grace of God.

Read these pages to rediscover the gift of a grace that saves, a connection that sustains, a holiness that is complete love of God, neighbor, and yourself. Trust that grace, connection, and holiness are our path to healing—perhaps your own healing, perhaps the healing of your congregation. And, dare we say it, perhaps the healing of The (United) Methodist Church.

For us this wholeness might seem impossible. The gospel does remind us that what is impossible for us is possible for God (Luke 1). And the good news? God is with us and for us. You are the dwelling place of God. And this is the gift of unrelenting grace.

One

Unrelenting Grace as God's Gift to Us

A Traditional Faith

In the Lord's Prayer (Matthew 6:9-13) we say the words "forgive us our sins, as we forgive those who have sinned against us." Where we have sinned against God and each other, through commission or omission, we ask forgiveness. And where we have been sinned against, we extend that same forgiveness.

By praying the Lord's Prayer in worship, we identify as persons with a traditional faith. The church of my preference would say the Lord's Prayer and the Apostles Creed (*UM Hymnal*, p. 881) in worship. We would sing more about God than ourselves. This would be true if you have a traditional faith, which is to say that your "convictional stance" (*Book of Discipline*, paragraph 427) is generously orthodox. Orthodoxy is rooted in the scriptures, creeds, and hymns that we teach. It is life-giving.

Generosity is essential because orthodoxy can also be used as a knife to separate and do harm. In this extended and complex season, many Methodists experienced the harm of having their faith described in less than charitable ways. And this characterization is used as justification for some (not all) of those who have departed.

A generously orthodox faith is deeply rooted in God's grace. That grace is for all of us. The parables of Jesus and stories about his life make this point repeatedly: the prodigal (Luke 15), the Samaritan (Luke 10), the great banquet (Luke 14), touching the person with a skin disease (Matthew 8), the woman at the well (John 4), the feeding of the five thousand (Matthew 14), the thief on the cross (Luke 23), and more.

We struggle with the meaning of *all*. At our best, we are not defined in either/or categories but are always a diverse collection of people.

> United Methodists all over the globe are liturgical, contemporary, charismatic, social activists, urban, suburban, small town, rural and much more. We are children, youth, young adults, senior adults, new Christians, and mature Christians. We are present

on four continents, in more than 45 countries, and we comprise an unknown number of cultures and languages. We are a holy communion of different races, ethnicities, cultures, and perspectives united by the Holy Spirit, driven by the mission of Christ, and bearing the good news of an unmerited grace that changes lives and transforms communities. ("The Bishops' Narrative for the Continuing United Methodist Church")

We have many differences, and they are important, and we do not suppress them, but they are not as important as the way Jesus sees us and embraces us on the cross and calls us to a lifelong journey of transformation (Matthew 4).

We struggle with all of this.

A United Methodist Way of Life

So who is the *we*?

We are United Methodists. There is a United Methodist way of life. It involves our response to the grace of God, in ourselves and others. It includes searching the scriptures and singing about the amazing love of God, so free, so infinite its grace ("And Can It Be," *UM Hymnal*, no. 363). It insists on our need for connection and social holiness. I can't be holy on my own; I can't be holy without you; you can't be holy without me.

This way of life understands holiness as love of God and love of our neighbor. This love draws us toward each other; it doesn't separate us from each other into groups of pure and impure people.

A United Methodist way of life is welcoming. At our best, we have welcomed persons from other denominations, from non-denominational churches, and from backgrounds without faith expression. Many have brought gifts to us. We continue to have distinctive gifts to offer to all who become a part of us.

A United Methodist way of life is rooted in prevenient grace: God is present in all, and every person is of sacred worth (*Book of Discipline*, paragraph 4). Such life is anchored in scripture, which means life is Christ-centered. It requires a convicted humility. We are on a lifelong journey to holiness, and we are not there yet. We see a reflection from a mirror (1 Corinthians 13:12).

We are connectional. We believe that institutions are important—they provide many of the things we need, especially for the most vulnerable. Our churches and institutions need innovation, reformation, and fresh expressions of church. The good news doesn't change. What changes are the ways people gather and grow and serve and understand themselves.

Deep and Disruptive Changes

We are in the grip of change, deep and disruptive change. Yet I'm convinced that we are on the way to being a better church. Much work has been done toward this improvement, in local congregations and in the global church.

Our prayer for departing Christian friends is that they will quickly move into the mission to which God calls them, without speaking in disparaging ways about our church and recruiting from within our churches; this is not their mission. Departing Christians have a mission, and it can be blessed by the Lord. There are orderly, transparent, and fair processes whereby persons and local churches can depart from the denomination. And to those who have chosen to depart, we are not enemies. We have a different vision for the church. And yet it is rooted in the soil of the same doctrine (*Book of Discipline*, paragraph 104), and in the most basic and most ancient creed: Jesus is Lord.

For those who continue as United Methodists, and this will be the great majority of us, we will live into the challenge of being an evangelical church that is inclusive of all people, that finds new and fresh ways to disciple people, and that does all of this within our core values of grace, connection, and holiness.

Challenges to Our Discipleship

Two facets of discipleship challenge us the most.

First, historic racism has plagued Methodism from the beginning and took institutional form in our separation and segregation. Our work—in creating the beloved community in each congregation, in our public witness to unjust laws, and in our systems of annual conferences that are becoming more equitable—is rooted in the recognition that racism is a sin and an obstacle to our sanctification and health as a church.

Second, is our recognition that lesbian, gay, bisexual, and transgender persons are not "LGBTQ issues" but real people in our own churches and families. We are each blessed by the same grace, saved by the same cross, on the same journey to holiness. Singling Methodists out for discrimination has been a fifty-year, costly human error.

The harm we Methodists have done to these two segments of persons is staggering. It calls us, me, to confession, and to a changed heart and life.

These are two unfinished and imperfect facets of our discipleship. We have no arrogance about precisely how we do this work of healing. But we witness that, in some churches, and in small groups within many more churches, there is a foretaste of it. God is blessing it because God created each of us, in all our variety, in the divine image (Genesis 1:27). As the Apostle Peter declared to those who would exclude others, God shows no partiality (Acts 10).

If this discipleship growth is to be meaningful, it will happen at the local level, in our church buildings but also beyond them, over meals, in our homes, in one-on-one conversations. We will meet this discipleship challenge as we reemerge from a pandemic where many died, many more became extremely ill, and all were disrupted. There is complexity about this trauma. We will need to be people of peace in all respects, people immersed in the scriptures, and people who remain connected in a world whose default is to divide us. That is precisely what it means to be a disciple of Jesus Christ for the transformation of the world in this present moment (*Book of Discipline*, paragraph 121). It is the rediscovery of a United Methodist way of life. It can be the gift God gives to us and the gift we offer to the world.

A United Methodist way of life is about grace, connection, and holiness. Gather to explore these three gifts together, for it is a journey.

The Abundance of God's Grace

Thomas Langford reflects on the grace of God:

> In a basic sense, grace is Jesus Christ. Grace is the specific expression of God's nature and will, an incarnate and continuing presence. From the center in Jesus Christ, implications radiate, ranging from the prevenient grace of God to justification, regeneration, assurance, sanctification, means of grace, and final glorification. The grace of God, expressed in and defined by Jesus Christ, becomes inclusive of life. (Langford, *Practical Divinity*, p. 41)

> Around this point—the grace of God in Jesus Christ— several attendant commitments form a tight nexus: biblical witness to Jesus Christ, vital experience of God in Christ as Savior and Sanctifier, commitment to human freedom and ethical discipleship, and the shaping of church life around missional responsibility. (Langford, *Practical Divinity*, p. 250)

We sketch first the abundance of God's grace in a Wesleyan framework.

Prevenient grace is the presence of God in all people, prior to our acceptance of faith or response to divine revelation. We believe that every person is created in God's image, that all persons are of "sacred worth," and surely this is consensus in the Wesleyan tradition for ministries with all people. Our doctrine of prevenient grace is the basis for the conviction that no one is outside God's love and God's saving activity.

How do we practice the reality of prevenient grace? The Uniting Church of Australia, which includes Methodists, adopted a Revised Preamble to their Constitution. In it they affirm that "the First Peoples had already encountered the Creator God."

In many gatherings we acknowledge the indigenous peoples who inhabited the land prior to our arrival. It is important, when we move into public spaces as representative lay and clergy ministers of the gospel, to remember that we do not take the grace of God into these spaces. God's grace is already present.

This is also true for an individual. One of my spiritual guides, the evangelist Bob Tuttle, would talk with me about the spiritual importance of faithful decisions made by our ancestors. Once, as we joined hands with a couple whose infant was to be baptized, Bob voiced in prayer, "When this child reaches the moment of claiming the faith for her own, let it be that for her it is like taking a very small step over a narrow stream." This narrow stream is the gift of prevenient grace in our lives.

Justifying grace is the gift of salvation, which is ours through faith and apart from any merit. The ground is indeed level at the foot of the cross. We are saved by God's grace because of faith. This salvation is God's gift. It's not something we possess. It's not something we did, of which we can be proud (Ephesians 2). Fleming Rutledge speaks of an active God who is "binding himself in an unconditional covenant, revealing himself in the calling of a people, self-sacrificing in the death of his Son, prodigal in the gifts of the Spirit, justifying the ungodly, and, indeed, offending the 'righteous' by the indiscriminate use of [God's] favor" ("A Generous Orthodoxy: A Statement of Purpose").

The assurance that we can trust in the faithfulness of God through Jesus Christ to save us from sin (Romans 5) was a strong emphasis in the Reformed tradition, one of the traditions that shaped and interacted with the Wesleyan heritage. This assurance led to the King James Version's phrase "justified by faith" (v. 1). Justification is acceptance of God's gift, which is accepting and reconciling us. Some disciples of Jesus can recall a particular time and place when the gift of acceptance became especially profound, and our response was to say yes to it. This may have occurred in a worship service or in a camp setting or on a retreat. For me, the gift of God's justifying grace became more and more evident as I read through the New Testament as a college student. The unfolding story of the gospel—Jesus as a person, as a teacher, as a healer, and as a savior, and the writings of the Apostle Paul that explored why this was so important—gradually had a profound personal implication for me. It was, in the language of John Wesley, "a sure trust and confidence" that this assurance was real, and in faith, itself a gift ("Almost Christian," *John Wesley's Sermons*, II, 5). I accepted this as good news.

Sanctifying grace is the journey toward holiness, our lifelong response to the gift of grace. As someone along the way noted, sanctifying grace is all that God does in us after we say Jesus is Lord! Here let's observe a simple truth: in our church we have no disagreements about the gifts of prevenient and justifying grace. All are created in God's image. Salvation is a gift that we accept in faith, and not the result of our works or righteousness.

Yet concerning holiness, our opinions and divisions begin to emerge. Some emphasize personal (or interior or cloistered) holiness: the inward journey. Others value social justice, the reign of God with all its public and structural implications: the outward journey. The former sometimes see holiness through the lens of personal purity or piety; the latter through the consequences of how it transforms communities and liberates those Jesus names, for example, in Luke 4. Yet, of course, holiness or grace are not bifurcated;

14

Wesley spoke most often of sanctification as the love of God and neighbor (Matthew 22).

God's grace is abundant. To flatten or limit grace is to cheapen it. To restrict grace is to deny its very essence. Grace is a gift to us, but certainly a gift to be shared, lest being called and chosen looks more like privilege (Isaiah 42). We are urged by the Apostle Paul not to accept the grace of God in vain (2 Corinthians 6). The grace we have received, we extend to others. I can't love God, whom I have never seen, if I don't love my sibling whom I have seen (1 John).

Means of Grace

The grace we receive is sustained by the *means of grace*. Means are spiritual practices, sacraments, rituals. Wesley called them the ordinary channels by which Jesus is present to us. While God is not restricted or restrained by a finite number of pathways, it is also scriptural that God chooses to meet us in particular ways—as we pray or read the scriptures or receive Holy Communion. Beyond these practices in our tradition are other pathways: singing our faith, sharing our testimony, being with the poor, finding accountability and support in a small group.

These practices can add up to a method for growing in grace, which can have wonderful implications. We see the sacred worth in ourselves and in others; we are reminded again and again of the mercy and grace of Jesus, who loved us and gave himself for us; and we seek to be more loving toward

God and neighbor, stranger, and enemy. As we become more loving, the image of God, having been scarred by sin, is renewed. The renewal is personal devotion and corporate worship, ethical discipleship, and missional responsibility.

The center of focus is Jesus Christ. We are in a lifelong journey that radiates with implications of every kind, but all grounded by grace in a calling to become more faithful like Christ.

The Energy of God's Love

I served as a church pastor for twenty-eight years, knowing and loving people with widely different convictions. Most pastors I have known could share a similar experience. And most members of the churches I have served know, in a deep way, the differences that occur, within even the smallest of gatherings. Yet we could say the creed together, and when using the words of Jesus, we could pray for each other. I then served a very large and diverse annual conference in an equally large and complex state for ten years, where everyone had voiced the same membership and ordination promises.

Could we hold the unity of the church together, for the sake of the mission Jesus wanted to accomplish through us? Could we rebuild lives shattered by natural disasters, invest in young adults sorting out their futures, join hands with the sick and grieving, and open our spaces when outdoor temperatures dropped?

Yes, we could.

But disruptive forces brought fragmentation to the unity. The blame game began. The other person did it, right? We tend to minimize the unity and maximize the differences.

None of this behavior tells a new story. John Wesley had a short list of what unites us: core beliefs about God and Jesus, the scriptures, and a life filled with, in his words, "the energy of love." Love of God, love of neighbor, love of enemy—love for all people. These are easy words to speak, harder to put into practice.

Our differences are mostly in the category of what Wesley called "opinions." Opinions are contrasted with *doctrines*. Opinions are about nonessential matters; doctrines are core convictions about God.

We each have opinions.

Our opinions differ.

And our opinions could be wrong.

Here is some good news for a world polarized by conflict and selfish desires: The church's unifying foundation is not your opinion and not mine. The church's one foundation is Jesus Christ our Lord. That is the core belief.

Then what did Jesus teach us? With whom did he associate? What was his mission? And what was his gift to you and me? A clear picture emerges in this passage from the first public sermon of Jesus (Luke 4:16-20):

Jesus went to Nazareth, where he had been raised. On the Sabbath he went to the synagogue as he normally did and stood up to read. The synagogue assistant gave him the scroll from the prophet Isaiah. He unrolled the scroll and found the place where it was written:

The Spirit of the Lord is upon me,
   because the Lord has anointed me.
He has sent me
to preach good news to the poor,
   to proclaim release to the prisoners
   and recovery of sight to the blind,
   to liberate the oppressed,
   and to proclaim the year of the Lord's favor.

He rolled up the scroll, gave it back to the synagogue assistant, and sat down. Every eye in the synagogue was fixed on him. He began to explain to them, "Today, this scripture has been fulfilled just as you heard it."

Most Methodist people will find a unity. Some will depart. We have much more in common than what divides us. Our unity is found most deeply in the shared mission given to us by Jesus.

Almost all of what divides us is *opinion*. Opinions are important. You probably love some of your opinions, and I love some of mine. But opinions were never intended to divide Christ's body. There's nothing holy about our opinions.

So yes, our work is to ask God for more experiences of unity and fewer experiences of division. And unity is for the sake of the mission.

Make us one with Christ,
   one with each other,
   and one in ministry to all the world.
   (A Service of Word and Table I, *UM Hymnal*, p. 10)

Fill us with the energy of your love.

The Heart of Religion

Methodist life was marked by a deep and authentic personal piety that led to a broad and uncompromising social involvement. Methodists were known for their prayers and for their commitment to the poor and disenfranchised. This commitment resulted in persistent efforts to build houses of prayer and worship as well as consistent efforts to visit the prisons, build schools and hospitals, and work for laws that moved toward a just and peaceful social order. Not everyone agreed with or applauded the way early Methodists lived, but it did not require many at any one place to make a difference. (Rueben Job, *A Wesleyan Spiritual Reader*, p. 193)

United Methodists, if we remain true to our origins, are shaped by a religion of the heart. The heart represents the essence of who we are, and that essence has everything to do with our creation in God's image and our calling to live fully into that identity. We know that identity to be love. A religion of the heart is a love for God who first loved us. This is expressed in a personal piety, or "works of piety," which are simply the methods we use to keep this love alive. All relationships require this kind of attention, and our relationship with God is no different. The absence of this intentionality leads to stubbornness in the relationship, which is defined in the Old Testament as a hardened heart. Spiritual methods and practices keep us in relationship with God, and they are a pathway toward a life shaped toward God's desires for us in this life.

This pathway always points toward social involvement, toward connection. Wesley clearly insisted that there is no holiness but social holiness. A religion of the heart is necessarily joined to another whose heart is aligned also with God. This alignment is John Wesley's calling in the sermon on "The Catholic Spirit." If my heart is aligned with yours, Wesley preached, give me your hand, and let us join in the work of God.

And what is God's work?

It is, in part, a broad and uncompromising social involvement. Rueben Job paints a vivid picture of this when encouraging us to reconnect with our originating purpose: to build houses of prayer and worship, to visit the incarcerated, to work for access to education and health care, and to lift our voices in shaping public policy. Ours is a "both-and" conjunctive faith. We see in these actions no either-or thinking; rather evangelism and service (or justice) are yoked on the same path. A United Methodist way of life, because it is a religion of the heart, is deeply motivated to see all persons as worthy of the life that our Creator desires for us. That life is salvation and healing, learning and liberation, human dignity, flourishing, and hope.

A United Methodist way of life in some contexts may be a minority voice. We may not be the dominant expression of how we live together as citizens, as neighbors, or as God's people. But, as Rueben Job noted, that is our birthright. We are to be the salt of the earth and the light of the world (Matthew 5). Not everyone shares the causes to which we commit, the values that motivate us, the particular way of life that we learned from the scriptures and through the faithfulness of early Methodists. We can be at peace with this status. "It did not require many at any one place to make a difference" (Job, *A Wesleyan Spiritual Reader*, p. 193).

This purpose could be our calling in the present moment: to remember more fully who we are, and to know that, as we embrace this, God will use us to make a difference.

Study Questions

1. When and how did God's grace first become an assurance for you? When have you seen evidence of God's grace in another person's life?

2. Read the parable of the prodigal son in Luke 15. In what ways might we consider The United Methodist Church to be like the prodigal son? In what ways is it like the son who remained at

home? How is it like the father who waited for the younger son and welcomed him home?
Have you seen someone being prevented from responding to God's invitation to follow and serve in The United Methodist Church?

3. Does your congregation encourage and embody social holiness that combines support for personal piety with social involvement? Does it emphasize one more than the other? What might be done to support a healthy alignment of both?

Two

Unrelenting Grace Connects Us to Each Other

To Stay in Connection

The United Methodist way of being a Christian isn't the only way. It isn't the easiest way. It isn't the superior way. It holds together two different realities, human and divine. First, we were created for relationships, and we flourish when we are in connection with each other. Second, we were created by and for God, and we desire communion with God.

Each of these realities is at the heart of the two greatest commandments affirmed by Jesus, that we love God and our neighbor (Matthew 22:34-40). And these two commandments are how John Wesley spoke of holiness and happiness.

It is significant that, for Wesley, Holy Communion is a "converting ordinance." Not every branch of the church, not every way of being Christian would see our presence at the Lord's table as a converting experience.

Thus we are in connection with sinners, imperfect people. We don't always love each other well. And our communion is with a God whom we don't always love completely. As we say in our prayer of confession, "We have not loved you with our whole heart."

The relationship is a gesture of grace to us, the bread and wine placed in our hands. It is unmerited favor. And so we say the ancient prayer, "cleanse the thoughts of our hearts, by the inspiration of your Holy Spirit, that we may perfectly love you" ("A Service of Word and Table I," *UM Hymnal,* p. 6). We receive communion with the hope that our imperfect, even disordered, loves will mature.

It is easy to be in communion with a God who sees all things in the way we see them. And it is easy to be in connection with people who love us, and who give us no reason not to love them.

United Methodism is not easy for this very reason. It keeps us in communion with a God whose ways are not our ways. And it keeps us in connection with people who challenge our happiness, and, to take it a step further, it keeps us in connection with people who are not obstacles to our holiness but whose differences are the way we learn the practices that move us closer to holiness, that is, perfection in love in this life.

This movement through completed love is precisely the way of the cross. For us, the cross is fused with the flame, the purifying work of the Holy Spirit. This is our United Methodist way of sanctification.

Patience and Peacemaking

Most of us want peace. Not everyone wants peace, but most of us want peace. The dissonance comes because there seems to be so little well-being. The Old Testament word is *shalom,* which indicates a sense of well-being. The present moment could be described in the words of the seventh-century prophet, who criticized priests who would go around insisting, "all is well, all is well, when in fact nothing is well [*shalom*]" (Jeremiah 8:11).

In the season of Advent in our churches, we light the candle of peace, we read the scriptures about peace, and we await the coming of the promised prince of peace.

> It was the dream of the prophets.
> > It was the hope of his parents.
> > It was the message of his preaching.
> > It was the legacy of his Passover.
>
> Peace. We want peace. But we know so little peace in our world, in our community, in our lives. ("Patience, Peace, and the Promise of God: A Christmas Message from Bishop Carter")

So, what do we do with this dissonance? How do we resolve it? One response is to say that we are not peaceable people, that we do not really care enough about each other's well-being to make it happen. It's as if we have not figured out a way to construct peace or make it a reality.

But this is not quite right. Because peace isn't something we can create or invent. And to go more deeply, we don't always really know what peace is, do we? Some people sentimentalize peace. Peace is like a warm blanket or a hot bath or a sedative. Some people compartmentalize peace. I think of some neighborhoods in Latin America I have walked through: to keep the peace, the walls are lined with cut glass bottles, the jagged edges exposed, to separate those inside from those outside. We do this in more subtle and sophisticated ways in the United States.

Could we have peace if we just built a gigantic wall? In the land where the prince of peace was born, his descendants on both sides have little experience of peace, although the vast multitudes of Palestinians and Israelis want peace. I have come to know and love the church in Northern Ireland, as those disciples have lived through generational divisions and the trauma of the "Troubles." And in my own country we have mastered the art of gerrymandering, creating siloes that insulate us from those who differ. Could we have peace if we just separated the people we like from the people we don't like?

Is that peace? It turns out that peace is something different.

Peace

Peace is a right relationship with God. And a right relationship with God always places us into a right relationship with each other. Or at least it creates the conditions for that relational work. We do not *make* a right relationship. God has already done that. God has already made peace with the world.

The early followers could look back at Jesus, in the same way the prophets looked forward, and they could see the peace that Jesus had made possible on this earth:

> But now, thanks to Christ Jesus, you who once were so far away have been brought near by the blood of Christ. Christ is our peace. He made both Jews and Gentiles into one group. With his body, he broke down the barrier of hatred that divided us. (Ephesians 2:13-14)

Jesus is our peace. Peace is not a human achievement. Peace is a gift from God. And here we find ourselves much closer to the prophets, much nearer to the people we meet in the Gospels. We are praying for this gift, eagerly awaiting this gift of peace.

The extended season of division in United Methodism has taught us a lesson. There was perhaps a time when we experienced divisions in the world, in the community, in the workplace, or perhaps in our families, and the church was a safe place in contrast to all of that. The hour of worship was our peace. The rituals within that worship—the prayers, the hymns, the music, the familiar surroundings—provided sanctuary.

This sanctuary has been one of the losses over the past years. The pandemic, political polarization, and disaffiliations disrupted our spiritual practices. We are still wrestling with the fragments of this change.

In Isaiah 40, the prophet speaks of a transition, of change. The season of punishment has ended; now is the time of restoration and renewal. Comfort the people with this good news, the prophet says. Go to the top of a mountain and shout it out for all to hear. Those who have been wounded are now the very ones who will comfort others.

In 2 Peter 3, there is a further reflection on this transition. A thousand years is like a day with God. The transition seems slow in coming. We wait for this gift, but it doesn't appear. We want this promised peace, but where is it? God isn't slow, the scripture reminds us, but God is patient because of our stubbornness and sinfulness. God wants us to repent. God is interested in our readiness to receive the gift. God is not slow, but God is patient.

Waiting with Patience

I'm not always patient. The season of Advent teaches patience and waiting, whether you are a five-year-old child obsessed with a special gift or a grandparent counting the days until reunion with family.

Waiting, as we see it in the people on the first pages of the Gospel, is waiting with a sense of a promise already begun in us. So waiting is never a movement from nothing to something. It is always a movement from "Zechariah . . . your wife Elizabeth is to bear you a son." To "Mary . . . Listen! You are to conceive and bear a son." (Luke 1:13, 31) People who wait have received a promise that allows them to wait. They have received something that is at work in them, like a seed that has started to grow. This is very important. We can only really wait if what we are waiting for is from something to something more. (Nouwen, "A Spirituality of Waiting")

Peace is the gift of God, and we wait for it, but the waiting isn't passive. Peter writes to the first followers of Jesus, "While you are waiting for these things to happen, make every effort to be found by him in peace—pure and faultless. Consider the patience of our Lord to be salvation" (2 Peter 3:14-15; see also Romans 14:19).

The very absence of peace in our world, in our churches, in our lives, the imperfect slowness of making all things right, has to do with the patience of God, allowing us to use our freedom in God's service, allowing us to use our abundance as the provision of God's blessing, allowing us to use our woundedness as instruments of God's healing.

We are able to wait for peace because we have glimpsed it here and there, now and then. For the follower of Jesus, the prince of peace, something is already growing in us, a hunger and a thirst for a new world, for a new church. We are "waiting with a sense of promise."

It was the dream of the prophets.

It was the hope of his parents.

It was the message of his preaching.

It was the legacy of his Passover.

It was the longing of his people.

It was the fulfillment of his promise.

Under Construction

My family spent a part of our lives in the mountains of Western North Carolina, where we served churches and have a home. In that region we came to know some of the Graham family. Ruth and Billy Graham were traveling through the Western North Carolina mountains one afternoon when they encountered several miles of road construction. There was one-lane traffic, there were detours, it was a little frustrating. Finally, they came to the end, and they saw a road sign. Ruth Graham turned to her husband and said, "Those words, on that road sign, that is what I would like to have printed on my tombstone." The words on the road sign read:

End of construction

Thanks for your patience

We are in a time of transition. We are on the way to a better church. It's a time of active waiting and patient peacemaking. And we wait with a sense of promise. Don't be demoralized if the world doesn't seem to be a very peaceful place. Don't be downcast if the church reflects the world. Don't be discouraged if anxiety rules within your heart and confusion pervades your mind.

Those who walked with God before us knew this same dissonance, and yet they listened for a harmony at the heart of the universe, they took the bread and the cup into their hands as grace, they continued to gather for worship with fellow pilgrims, all of them, all of us without exception, under construction. Through it all they discerned a truth that was the joy of human desiring. They dreamed about a peace the world could neither give nor take away, a gift about to be revealed to us.

So, what do we do with our dissonance? How do we resolve it? God is not slow, but God is patient.

> There is still a vision for the appointed time;
>   it testifies to the end; it does not deceive.
> If it delays, wait for it;
>   for it is surely coming; it will not be late.
>   (Habakkuk 2:3)

Discipleship Is Reconciliation

I grew up in a medium-sized city in the deep South. We lived near my grandparents, and I sat in worship between my grandfather and my mother. It was not a Methodist church.

During middle school, my parents' marriage ended. They were good people, they were doing the best they could, and yet the marriage ended. Each of them has passed in recent years. In the aftermath of the divorce, two or three women from the church talked with my mother and said, in effect, it might be best if she found another church.

Consider that on the pew where we sat my grandparents' names were printed on a little plaque. And on the stained glass to our left their names were also remembered. They were not wealthy people, but they tithed. They gave ten percent of their income to the church.

And so we had a season of not being in church. In a deep South, Bible Belt culture, it was awkward. Months went by. Then a teacher, a friend to my mother, invited us to their Methodist Church.

It didn't have beautiful music. It didn't have a large and enthusiastic youth ministry. It was tucked back into a neighborhood, and it didn't have a strategic and visible location. I can't remember any of the sermons.

It did have what we most needed. It was a church of people with enough love to share with a new family, a somewhat broken and chaotic family.

And that is how I became a United Methodist. I now know that my unconscious bias is that we are not in the business of asking anyone to leave, or, as a wise friend said recently, giving people more reasons not to come to church. We don't have that luxury.

The Agenda of God

It also turns out that God has a very different agenda, and indeed one that seeks to include us and all people.

The gospel is at the core of our faith, and the Sermon on the Mount is at the core of the gospel. Many of the Standard Sermons that John Wesley gave to the early Methodists were from the Sermon on the Mount. These sermons begin with the Beatitudes, how life is blessed, how we flourish, what happiness means. Reading these first few verses of Matthew 5 is a reversal of the world's values. Disciples of Jesus are the salt of the earth, the light of the world. There is something different and distinct about a follower of Jesus. "You shall know the truth and the truth shall make you odd," which is an unconfirmed saying attributed to Flannery O'Connor. And then a statement that Jesus has not come to abolish the Old Testament— this is not out with the old, in with the new!—but he has come to fulfill the Law and the Prophets. And then the six antitheses: "You have heard it said, but I say to you." Jesus is giving us a model for a higher righteousness.

Jesus begins his instruction with teaching concerning murder, violence, and anger. If we go a little deeper, we recall the wisdom that the ancestor of anger is anxiety. We live in an anxious time, full of mass murders, vigilante assaults, angry mobs, fear of others, and worsening climate. We live in a deeply divided, profoundly anxious moment.

So how are we to be the church, a church that hears the voice of Jesus and the New Testament? What are we called to say, and who are we called to be?

The answer begins with you and me. Before you place your gift on the altar, Jesus says, first be reconciled to your brother or sister (Matthew 5:23-34).

Revival as Reconciliation

Early in ministry, I served a rural four-point charge in Yadkin County, North Carolina. A four-point charge is four churches who share a pastor and live in harmony—or something like that. I would discover that some of my most important spiritual teachers were members of these churches.

Every fall and spring, each church would have a revival, with services that would last several days. This meant I had eight weeks of revival a year. I was a very revived person! The stated purpose of these revival services was to reach and save the lost. They began on Sunday morning and continued Sunday evening through Wednesday or Thursday evening. So I would be listening to the visiting preacher on or about Wednesday evening, and the message would be about the lost and how they and we need to be found, and I would look out at the congregation and think, these people are not lost. They are the committed core. After all, they are here on the third or fourth night of a revival.

I wondered: Why do we have all these services? What is the purpose? After some time, it was as if God spoke to me and said, this is what is happening: When you live in a small community, no one new ever moves in or moves out. You go to school together, you do business with each other, families blend, things happen. We do harm to each other. Other people we know do harm to us. They do harm to people we love. If you live long enough, it happens, even in the best of families.

We begin to construct walls, right down the middle between us. This is where the revival services came in. In those services we were being called to make things right with each other. So people would come forward, and they would kneel at the altar, and they would make peace with their Creator and with someone—a neighbor, family member, a business partner—they would make peace, and they would leave it there at the altar. It was reconciliation.

What would it mean, in a culture and in a church divided in most every way, for us to be the outlier, the exception? How do we do that?

First be reconciled, Jesus says.

Reconciliation and Racism

In the Old Testament, and still the holiest day in Judaism, the annual equivalent to these revivals is the Day of Reconciliation (Yom Kippur), which John Tyndale translated as Day of Atonement (at-one-ment).

The Greek word for reconciliation, *katallage*, occurs rarely in the New Testament—it appears four times, all in the letters of Paul (though a related word does appear in Matthew). It is not a word commonly used in Greek religious discourse; it had more to do with settling political disagreements. Matthew and Paul apply the word to our relationship with God and what God is calling us to do and be. Paul writes, in 2 Corinthians 5:18, "God . . . reconciled us to himself through Christ and has given us the ministry of reconciliation" (NRSVue).

A few years ago, I was with a group that met several members of the Mother Emmanuel African Methodist Episcopal Church in Charleston, South Carolina. The AME Church came into being when Richard Allen, a prominent Black leader, was asked to leave The Methodist Church in Philadelphia in 1787. Richard Allen was later ordained by Francis Asbury in 1799 and consecrated a bishop by Asbury in 1816.

Emmanuel Church was planted in Charleston during this time. It is the oldest Black church of any kind in the South. In 1822, it was burned to the ground because it had become a center of teaching and preaching about liberation and freedom among slaves. It was rebuilt, and it was and is a vital church.

In 2015, a young man drove two hours to Charleston, went into the church on a Wednesday night, and took part in the Bible study. At the conclusion of the Bible study, everyone stood and closed their eyes in prayer. In the next few seconds, the young man fired seventy-four bullets from a semiautomatic weapon, killing nine people, including the pastor.

We listened to their story, and at the end we all walked to the altar. At the time I tried to imagine the grief of the people who worship there. I have since wondered: what is God calling me to do, to understand how I need to be a part of the solution to the pain and the injustice and the unrighteousness and the deadly toxicity. First be reconciled, Jesus says. Turn the other cheek. Go the extra mile. Love your enemies.

Jesus is teaching what he will come to embody. "God . . . reconciled us to himself through Christ. . . . So we are ambassadors for Christ" (2 Corinthians 5:18, 20 NRSVue). God is making the appeal through us. This is the end of 2 Corinthians 5. And then Paul continues, in the next chapter:

> We are also begging you not to receive the grace of God in vain. He says, *I listened to you at the right time, and I helped you on the day of salvation.* Look, now is the right time! Look, now is the day of salvation! (2 Corinthians 6:1-2)

Reconciliation, Salvation, and Holiness

For Wesleyans, our salvation has holiness as its end or completion: Wesley called it "Christian perfection." The end of Matthew 5:48 has a simple statement of Jesus: "Be perfect, therefore, as your heavenly Father is perfect" (NRSVue). In Luke's Gospel, the parallel teaching has it

37

this way: "Be merciful, just as your Father is merciful" (6:36 NRSVue). Both imperatives are concluding words that the early church heard Jesus saying after his instructions to first be reconciled, to turn the other cheek, to go the extra mile, to love our enemies. Be complete in showing love. Be merciful. Be perfect.

They are two words that provoke a similar theme: What if perfection (complete love) is mercy and mercy is perfection?

I have stood many times before the altar and raised my hands to God and said the words of invocation that the Holy Spirit would be present in the bread and cup that we receive, and that we would actually be the body of Christ for the world. And then we make the powerful request of God:

> Make us one with Christ, (this is faithfulness)
> make us one with each other, (this is unity)
> and make us one in ministry to all the world. (this is
>   fruitfulness)

We share the table to see that the work of the Holy Spirit does sustain ordinary people, that is all of us, in our daily attempts to represent Christ wherever we are. The faithfulness, unity, and fruitfulness of the church form a whole. We can't be one without abiding in Jesus; we can't be Spirit-filled without loving our neighbor; we can't experience revival as we sow divisions in the body, which is the church.

Many churches have a practice of setting aside a Sunday during the year for young people to share the message and lead in worship. This was my experience and gift in several congregations. Members of the youth would share the message of the gospel, what the church had taught them, and how they were integrating the faith with what they knew of themselves while growing up in a Christian community.

Some of them as adults now identify as queer persons. I want them to know this reconciliation, the complete and perfect love. Most of us see their sacred worth. We can be reconciled. They are a part of this family, and unlike that conversation with my mother, we simply can't say to them, "It might be best if you found another church."

Eventually, in her last years, my mother returned to the church that had asked her to leave. Whenever I visited, we would go to that church. I recognize now that her return to that space, as difficult as it might have been for her, was her own way of teaching me about reconciliation.

"God . . . reconciled us to himself through Christ." That is our personal salvation. And God has given us the ministry of reconciliation. That is how we work out our salvation with each other. You can't pull all of that apart. It is finally one gift, one gospel.

Both Matthew 6 and 2 Corinthians 5 are about what we do with our gift. That gift is the grace of God. We urge you, Paul says, not to accept the grace of God in vain.

The revival preachers got something right. There is an urgency. "Come to terms quickly," Jesus says. This is a conversation that mature disciples need to have with each other. It is a conversation the Lord wants to have with us.

Right now, discipleship is reconciliation, and reconciliation is discipleship.

The Scriptures and How We Read Them

Along the way, some have said to us, "The Bible is really simple, isn't it?" Or "The Bible is really clear about this." As a person who loves the Bible, who has spent a lifetime teaching, preaching, and seeking to live under its guidance, upon reflection this simplification may not be as true as we would wish.

Why might that be? The scriptures are a collection of divinely inspired writings—a library of scrolls—including instruction, law, gospel, songs, narratives, poetry, wisdom, and prophecy. And within the scriptures there are narratives and counter-narratives: for example, Isaac and Ishmael, Sarah and Hagar. Our narratives shape our identities, and our identities are also formed in the groups of which we are a part, groups that tell us their stories and how to interpret them.

Narratives and Counter-Narratives

We read the same scriptures and yet can differ in our interpretations. So what if covenant and love are potential narratives and counter-narratives in scripture. Is the cross covenant or love, or both? And what if liberation and orthodoxy are potential narratives and counter-narratives in scripture. Is the cross liberation or orthodoxy, or both?

What if narratives are the stories we are most likely to tell about ourselves, given our life experience and place in the world, and counter-narratives are the stories that we are less likely to see or more likely to miss?

Can a progressive see the covenantal beauty in a conservative person? Can a conservative see the passion for the marginalized in a progressive person?

If we belong to a group that is formed by one narrative, we may move toward seeing the truth in the other group's narrative. Yet, as Rabbi Jonathan Sacks notes, "In situations of stress, sympathy for the other side can be seen as betrayal" (Sacks, *Not in God's Name*, p. 118).

Thus we revert to our tribes. Sadly, in this season of division and disaffiliation, this tribal tendency has been the experience of almost every local church, every Sunday school class, every small group and committee, every collection of friendships.

How do we struggle and wrestle with the scriptures that have narratives and counter-narratives within them? We can say that our identities are shaped by the scriptures, but they are also shaped by the groups to which we belong.

The challenge comes when our interests—our well-being, even our salvation—are clear, but counter-narratives conflict with our identities. An even greater dissonance emerges when we grasp that our salvation is bonded with the salvation of others. So we find ourselves doing things against our own interests because of our (group) identity.

This is self-destructive, but it does avoid the pain of risking disappointment or rejection from our own group.

How we interpret scripture led to our present divisions and is a question we must wrestle with in the continuing United Methodist Church. Thankfully, we have a resource that can be helpful to us. It is a resource we have neglected, like treasure hidden in a field.

The Quadrilateral

As a people seeking to be led by God, our language about scripture in the Doctrinal Standards (*Book of Discipline*, paragraph 104) and Our Theological Task (paragraph 105) is instructive.

The scriptures contain all things necessary for salvation (Article 5, Methodist Church, and Article 4, Evangelical United Brethren). The Confession of Faith adds that the scripture is received through the Holy Spirit as "the true rule and guide for faith and practice." The Ministry of the Word is named among the ordinances of God in the "General Rules" (paragraph 104), as is searching the scriptures. We understand scripture both critically and devotionally, both corporately and individually.

Scripture is the primary source for doctrine, and yet it can be grasped only in relation to tradition, experience, and reason, which some teach as a *quadrilateral* (four-sided) method for interpreting the biblical books, a term coined by theologian Albert Outler. Indeed, scripture includes within itself a diversity of traditions, individual and corporate experiences, and the instrumentality of reason.

Tradition is the awareness of historical continuities between the ancient text and the present moment. It honors the reality that the Holy Spirit continues to speak, comforting and correcting. There is both a consensus in tradition and an ever-expanding attention to voices who have been muted and suppressed.

Religious *experience* for Wesley was strongly related to what he described "as sure trust and confidence" in God's gift of forgiveness, salvation, and new life. At the same time, experience encompasses the aspirations of all for equality and liberation. Experience is connected to everyday human realities, how scripture is in dialogue with our common and shared life.

Reason is closely related to our search for clarity and coherence, our conviction that all truth originates in God, and the legitimacy of a questioning mind that seeks to know the mind and will of God.

As a source in the Doctrinal Standards, *scripture* is described briefly. In the Theological Task, scripture is understood in a more nuanced and expanded way. After vigorous theological debate, we have a more nuanced view of the quadrilateral as constituted by scripture, tradition, reason, and experience. John Wesley's own heritage saw scripture as a primary source but not an exclusive source; as an Anglican, Wesley taught *prima scriptura*, not *sola scriptura* (Scripture first but not Scripture alone).

The Dialogue of Reading Scripture

The question is how to see these four sources of insight in relation to each other. Many have noted the limitations of seeing them rigidly or geometrically. Albert Outler would later regret coining the use of the metaphor, in that the image was interpreted or criticized too literally, even as the historical and situational practice was present in the life and thought of Wesley.

Billy Abraham criticized the quadrilateral as a vehicle for limiting the authority of scripture. John Cobb noted that the quadrilateral makes essential space for the (present) reality of human experience and reason in relation to the (past) resources of scripture and tradition.

Randy Maddox was convinced that the four sources of insight are in dialogue with each other, restoring an insight of Outler's. Maddox and Russ Richey spoke of the four sources as conferring with each other, which is an analogy with our Methodist practice of conferencing, when we seek as human beings with limited understandings to understand God's will in corporate gatherings.

How might the four sources of interpretation become a more constructive resource in the way we go about conferencing, recognizing that the sources themselves confer with each other?

I have come to see the inadequacy of reading scripture in a static way, claiming its priority and yet ignoring the very real way that the other sources of influence are inherent in the way I understand and begin to speak about a scripture passage. I have also come to an increasing appreciation for the mystery of scripture, for the diversity of traditions—narratives and counter-narratives—that are found there, and for the astonishing power of the Holy Spirit to bring scripture to human life (in renewal movements and in liberation movements, for example).

If the quadrilateral is a way that sources of insight confer with each other, it might help to define *confer* (Latin *conferre*). *Con* (with) implies the state of being together, and *ferre* is to bring, to hear, to suffer, to endure. The four sources (scripture, tradition, reason, experience) confer with each other in their integrity, until there is a consensus that honors each to the greatest possible degree or hears each voice without suppressing it.

To love the scriptures and to read them in community with each other and with the awareness that we come to them as conferencing people is essential to healing our United Methodist hearts. This reminds me of the profound insight of Chimamanda Adichie in her "Danger of a Single Story," where she concludes that to hear one another's stories is a "kind of paradise"!

As a Christian, I can honor those who see or think in ways that are different from me. At my best, I listen to others and learn from them. I have less ability to know the right response to those who don't enter the conversation, perhaps because they see the answer as simple and obvious. As a friend told me, God is not simple. God is Trinity. God is mystery. God is infinity. And God is a cross.

We will never grasp all there is of God in this life; we will never arrive at the status of holiness, even as we journey toward it. Add to this the mystery of human sexuality. Add to this my desire for power and control and privilege. Add to this my distorted vision and my heart turned in on itself (sin).

The good news: God overcomes all this. God created me, justifies me, even sanctifies me, but not apart from those who differ from me, and, I believe, not apart from the church, which is surely no more or less flawed than I am. God is never finished with me, or with any of us, until we see God face to face.

How can we read and teach Scripture in a way that isn't used as a weapon, which does violence, but as a means through which God restores us?

Here is a simple prayer for healing, because in all of this we rely on a wisdom greater than our own:

> O God,
> Hear the cries of all who long
>   to be a part of your great story.
> Remove our fears and distorted understandings
>   of each other.
> And give us a renewed vision of every tribe
>   gathered before your throne and the Lamb of God,
>   who takes away the sin of the world. Amen.

How We See Each Other: A Third Way

There is often some kind of impasse between a couple in marriage or two parties in an employment issue, or two people who view an "ism" differently, or (at least) two perspectives in a denomination. Peacemakers search with people in a variety of circumstances for some kind of "third way."

A third way in negotiation theory is often related to mutual benefit, exploring ways we can expand the benefits to those who differ. It is never about splitting the difference, as there are simply some matters about which we can't find a compromise that appeals to our conscience.

The only fruitful way to explore compromise of conscience is to consider the various ways we make space for difference and the ways we do not. For example, in the organizing *Book of Discipline of The United Methodist Church,* two matters were declared to be incompatible with Christian teaching—homosexuality (paragraph 161) and war (paragraph 165). Some have not made space for difference regarding sexuality, but in war we have made space for those who serve in the military and those who are conscientious objectors.

In my family tree, people I love have served in the military, and people I love are conscientious objectors. They each have something to teach me. I could not imagine my life or heritage without any of them.

In local churches, friends often find themselves on different sides of very important matters in the local community. The body of Christ would not be whole without them.

How is this possible? Well, you could say, with the Apostle Paul, when it comes to knowledge "I see only a dim reflection in a mirror" (1 Corinthians 13:12; KJV: "see through a glass darkly"). All of us have found ways to adapt our consciences to the realities that come our way. Every one of us has done this, without exception. So we search for a third way about most any matter that is of importance to us.

We are discovering what a third way is *not*. A third way isn't avoidance. A third way isn't to go silent or to say, "Let's not talk about it, let's change the subject, let's leave this for someone else to work on later."

A third way must fully appropriate the concerns of all who are at the table, who seek a solution, in the hope that there is some facet of this dispute that has not yet occurred to us.

We have not yet arrived at a place of certainty on many complex subjects. Clarity, perhaps. Certainty, no. This caution is related to the concept of convicted humility. I can hold and love my convictions, and yet I can believe, this side of heaven, there is more truth and light to be revealed to me.

This deliberation is the work of the Holy Spirit, which will guide us into all the truth (John 16). The Spirit is creative, mysterious, and beyond our control, as are many of the matters that divide us. I am convinced that just underneath the surface of our most adamant stance lies a struggle that we would prefer to put to rest. Yet that is God's unfinished agenda with us.

Think for a moment about all of those who are in parishes, conversations, families, friendships, and leadership roles. Give thanks for the astonishingly different gifts. Give thanks for who you are, and for the convictions that are shaping you. And then imagine that you are a work in progress. I know that I am.

The search for a third way is about confidence in all of this, that God who began a good work (of perfecting love) in you will be faithful to complete it (Philippians 1).

The missiologist Dana Robert spoke to an annual conference whose theme was "On Mission Together." She noted that the word *together* might be what is hardest for us! The practice of Holy Communion, the virtue of patience, the call to peacemaking and reconciliation, an awareness of how we read scripture, and a search for a "third way" beyond simplistic divisions: these are some of the resources for strengthening our connection as United Methodists and as followers of Jesus.

This work is essential, because our connection exists for a greater purpose: the mission of sharing in God's unrelenting grace for the world.

Study Questions

1. Whom do you love with your whole heart? Who is hard to love with your whole being?

2. What trauma or opinions disrupt peace in your church?

3. How does your church wrestle with those scriptures about which there are multiple viewpoints or competing narratives? What books, stories, or passages in scripture does your church wrestle with the most? How do you listen to and encourage contrary interpretations?

4. Connection is an institutional metaphor in a Methodist way of life. Why is connection so challenging to sustain during periods of trauma and disruption?

5. Can you describe the "third way" of negotiating peace? How have you sought (or how might you seek) this third way when it comes to your family? Your church?

Three

Unrelenting Grace
Is God's Way of Life
in the World

Personal and Social Holiness

What is personal holiness and what is social holiness? Personal holiness is paying attention to and cultivating a relationship with God, who has long been in relationship with us. From our side, we develop a relationship with God through prayer, scripture reading, and participation in worship. At the heart of worship for Methodists is the practice of singing our faith and the frequent sharing of Holy Communion.

A prayer in the Anglican tradition, which was well known to John Wesley, we call the Collect for Purity. These words were a part of his prayer book, although they can be traced to the eleventh century.

> Almighty God,
> To you all hearts are opened, all desires known,
>   and from you no secrets are hidden.
> Cleanse the thoughts of our hearts
>   by the inspiration of your Holy Spirit
>   that we may perfectly love you
>   and worthily magnify your holy name.

This prayer teaches that God knows us intimately, with an echo of Psalm 139. It speaks of God's desire to cleanse us (see Psalm 51) through the ongoing work of the Holy Spirit. This renewal is for making us more perfect in love toward God, and for offering praise and glory to God.

Holy people practice inward spiritual disciplines. But holiness is also marked by a collective responsibility for others, especially the most vulnerable. Both private and collective piety identify United Methodists as people of the cross and the flame.

Toward the end of his life, Jonathan Sacks, the chief rabbi of England, reflected on the question, "Am I my brother or sister's keeper?" He defined responsibility as not only obligation but also righteousness. He then referred to Noah, who built the ark, "as a righteous man in a fur coat," and then made the distinction: "There are two ways of keeping warm on a cold night. You can wear a fur coat or light a fire. Wear a fur coat and you warm yourself only. Light a fire, and you warm others. We are supposed to light a fire" (Sacks, "Righteousness Is Not Leadership").

United Methodists are in connection with each other to light a fire. God has used the ordinary people of our church to save countless persons from death by malaria, to rebuild countless homes and lives after natural disasters, to make it possible for boys and girls to attend camp and receive an education. God has used clergy to preach the gospel and share the grace of the sacraments. God has used laity to bring light and hope into families, workplaces, and communities.

In our connection, we light a fire. We are the people of the cross and the flame. The cross that saves us, the flaming Spirit that kindles in us the fire of God's love, is the integration of personal and social holiness.

It is our way of life.

The Gifts We Can Bring: Building an Institutional Home for the Future

Jane Marshall expresses it this way in "What Gift Can We Bring":

> What words can convey it, the joy of this day?
>   When grateful we come, remembering, rejoicing
>   (*UM Hymnal*, no. 87)

For the moment, after setting aside the convictions and ideologies that are at the heart of our continuing differences as The United Methodist Church (and of course these cannot be set aside), we will soon enough enter the experience of being a different denomination. Some of us are energized by this. Some have departed, some will depart soon, some later. They have signaled this to us. Among these will be some of our friends. There is undeniable grief and loss. Others have done extended harm to many among us, especially the most vulnerable. We will find ways and rituals to care for these departures and losses.

We all know that "the long goodbye" has brought forth an extended diversion and withholding of gifts. Many who are departing have invested significant time, energy, and financial resources in imagining an alternative denomination or an independent congregation. A number of these have been in leadership roles: boards, committees, cabinets, the Council of Bishops, pastors of local churches. Some have withheld connectional giving. Certainly, many have withheld public encouragement and support when the denomination has been engaged in needed and honorable mission. Among these, many have a long pattern of channeling resources toward nondenominational ministries, whether these be mission or evangelism or education.

These designations are not necessarily bad, but the diversion points to a reality: we have not been channeling the fullness of our gifts toward a common life, toward building up the body or strengthening the connection, toward what a mentor once called "the community woodpile." Our hope for the near and longer term is that we will consciously focus on the question of how we add our gifts to a continuing United Methodist Church after separation.

Some currently in The United Methodist Church clearly desire a different or nondenominational context in which to do ministry. This is their choice and their work, not ours. They withhold gifts because they see no lasting home here. Some who are currently in the UMC are ambivalent. They are waiting to see how their own leadership fits into either the United Methodist or Global Methodist or a nondenominational identity. They are "on the fence." A much smaller number of persons will remain in the UMC simply to do harm through disparagement. This characterization would be one differentiation between the Global Methodist Church, which departs, and the Wesleyan Covenant Association, which remains.

Our primary agenda is to create a culture where we are contributing our gifts to The United Methodist Church. For all laity, for younger persons, for persons of color, for women in ministry, and for gay, lesbian, bisexual, and transgender participants, this agenda means creating opportunities for leadership, and underneath that, the assurance that all are seen. Persons who have been in leadership for some time are called to be a bridge between what has been—and here we come with gratitude, remembering, rejoicing—and what will be. Some of us will not live fully into the latter space, but there are extraordinary resources of talent and sufficient resources of financial capital to make, mold, and shape the continuing United Methodist Church into a vital branch of the One Body.

To build a bridge into this new future, we would be freed from binary opposites that seek some small advantage, the "caustic collusion" named in *The Anatomy of Peace* (Arbinger Institute). We need to name inappropriate behavior and speech from the outset should persons remain within the church with the primary task of undermining the continuing United Methodist Church. There is no reason to believe that some of the more extreme political groups will not do this. Their motivations are less religious or orthodox than they are political in pursuit of power, in essence, to destabilize institutions.

Why is this important?

We will need to contribute gifts because our institution will be in a new place. No one *loves* institutions, and yet we need the goods and benefits that institutions provide, among these: support for full-time set-apart ministry, resources for response to growing human needs, and additional support for the sustaining of leadership after a season of trauma. We know there is a lowered trust in institutions across the social spectrum. Yet most of those who will read this reflection, including entire congregations, are invested in institutions for the reasons named.

Here is a note of optimism. The departure of those withholding the gifts of their time, energy, and even their calling will create an important space for those who lead in the continuing United Methodist Church. We will need to lay aside the ways in which we have become addicted to or (to use Edwin Friedman's word) *enmeshed* in the oppositional fight. We will need to channel at least some of our deconstructionist leanings toward the construction of something new. Those in longer-term leadership must walk alongside (and not withdraw) but take our cues from those who will have many more years to serve and lead. These younger leaders also possess a wisdom about the mission field we are not now reaching. Our learning here will be an example of reverse mentoring.

We trust that the next wave of leaders will design and build a house that they themselves will live in. Consider Wesley's description of the porch, the door, and the house. The house will be where we are being perfected in love, which involves purging the *isms* as a necessary and essential part of loving our neighbor because we love God.

A part of our journey includes seeing our sacred spaces in different ways. Our buildings are important to us, but the church is not a building. The church is a people. Many of our disagreements are, on the surface, about buildings. We will need to move beyond these conversations, make our peace with property, building, and structure, and see the new thing that God is preparing for us. That new thing is what God is also calling us to invest in: our prayers, our presence, our gifts, our service, our witness.

The next generation's church will be about justice and mercy rooted in discipleship and spirituality as the redefined path to sanctification. It will be grounded in the core values of grace, connection, and holiness. This church will need leaders, teachers, missionaries, spiritual directors, pastors, lay leaders, trainers, servants, and builders. It will flourish as the people who remain—who will be most of us—ask and respond to the question, "What gift can I bring?"

Provoked to Love

In contrast to a focus on the opinions that divide, Wesley simply asked to be "provoked to love" (Hebrews 10:24 KJV). As we build up each other, as we are open to instruction in how to be more loving, as we seek not our own will but the divine will, as we are open to amending our faults, we become persons whom God can use for a particular service that is needed now.

Jesus was asked what is the greatest commandment in the *Torah* (law)? He responded:

> You must love the Lord your God with all your heart, with all your being, and with all your mind. This is the first and greatest commandment. And the second is like it: You must love your neighbor as you love yourself. All the Law and the Prophets depend on these two commands. (Matthew 22:36-41)

We always read the scriptures within our contexts and alongside our life experiences. It is important to name the recent history we have navigated.

- Many millions have died in the global pandemic of COVID.
- There has been a recurrence of racially motivated shootings and other hate crimes.
- We witnessed a violent transition of presidential power in the United States (and elsewhere), and elections are increasingly polarized.
- These realities affect how employees work or do not work and how students go to school or are unable to do so.
- Frontline workers (such as servers, drivers, and day-care providers) and helping professionals (such as nurses, teachers, spiritual leaders) experience increasing demands on their mental and physical well-being.
- Businesses small and large are disrupted.
- Important ritual events have often been canceled, postponed, or greatly diminished.

In an extended season of crisis and chaos, we seek a place to stand, a path to follow, a light to guide us.

Love God

Very simply in this traumatic season, we discover or rediscover what it means to love God and love neighbor. We engage in the spiritual practices of intercession (praying for others) and of gratitude (for the provision of our needs), and of trust in God as our higher power.

We read the scriptures, immerse ourselves in particular passages that have sustained us in the past, and acquaint ourselves with the diverse narratives that constitute this holy book. We search the scriptures for answers, or at least better questions. We recall particular, life-giving phrases:

> He leads me beside still waters.
>
> Peace I leave with you.
>
> Come to me, all of you who labor
> and carry heavy burdens, and I will give you rest.
>
> God so loved the world.

And we worship God in the sanctuary, perhaps online. The line of a hymn touches us. A fragment of the Lord's Prayer resonates. We touch the offering plate and place something in it. We receive the bread and the cup. We pass the peace. We kneel at an altar.

Through it all, we love God, or, to say it more intimately, we fall in love with God, or stay in love with God. The love of God is within the pain, loss, and grief. Yet, we love God.

What provokes us to love God? It is surely the remembrance that we love because God first loved us. Our love is a response to the gift. Prayer, reading scripture, and worship center us in the great narrative of that gift. And as deliberate Christians, we have an innate sense that we need a method that puts us in a place and time to receive the gift. It might be praying each day, or worshiping each Lord's Day, or reading through the Bible in a year, or receiving Holy Communion as often as possible.

We are provoked to love God as we come home to our true selves, persons created in God's image, who have a spiritual hunger for communion.

Our recent history disrupted all of this: pandemics and polarization and disaffiliation and loss and struggle. Yet we are provoked to love God and to reassemble for this purpose. Not as our ought. As our gift to each other. As a remembrance of who we are.

Love Our Neighbor

What does it mean to love our neighbor in this season? We have come through a global pandemic, which persists. In the deepest part of that experience, this meant keeping a social distance, so that we could flatten the curve of the spread of the virus and, in addition, so that we might protect the most vulnerable. It meant wearing a mask, which would become a politically divisive sign, and yet also an outward and visible sign of the love of neighbor.

To love our neighbor is also to confess that Black Lives Matter. In this way our love takes the form of justice, and we are taking a step closer to the fulfillment of our baptismal promises, to resist evil, injustice, and oppression in whatever forms they present themselves.

We love our neighbors as we are generous with others. If I have an abundance, or even a sufficiency, I share that with others. Our world and our nation are marked by profound economic disparities. Our Wesleyan heritage is deeply shaped by the outstretched hand toward children in poverty, the sick, those without housing, the unemployed, and those without access to education. In the practice of generosity, we discover the mutuality of giving and receiving, and our eyes are opened to the gifts of those without material privilege.

Consider a parable about a group of women and men who were touring a spacious and beautiful mansion. They paused in the great room of the house, and the guide drew the attention of all to an exquisite chandelier above them.

They continued the tour and minutes later made their way through a narrow hallway, which was illumined by a single bulb. Later one in the group commented, "That single bulb probably kept more people from stumbling than the great chandelier."

In a time of disruption, complexity, and chaos, we discover small and yet significant ways to love our neighbor.

Love Yourself

We love the neighbor, Jesus said, as we love ourselves. What could this mean for us?

We extend grace to ourselves; we have been living and leading through multiple complexities. We spend time with ourselves. This is about introspection, silence, and self-reflection. While the contexts were certainly different, recall the persons throughout history who lived in circumstances of constraint, criticism, and harm: Martin Luther King Jr., Dostoevsky, Nelson Mandela, Anne Frank, the Apostle Paul.

Many leaders in the church, both laity and clergy, have engaged in very active lives. Over time, we needed to become less active and more reflective. The opportunity for us is to know ourselves more fully and deeply.

It is enough in an extended season of complexity to define faithfulness as the daily practice of loving God and loving our neighbor as we love ourselves. This is the first and greatest commandment that Jesus gave us. Again and again, this is the way John Wesley defined the path to holiness. This can be a way of life for us, to be provoked to love.

This provocation ties together love in its fullness. God is gracious toward us. God's grace overflows in community and connection. God's grace is present in the world beyond us, awaiting our awareness. To love God is to love our neighbor, to experience love from that same neighbor, and to love ourselves, again in the awareness that we are all of us created in the image of God.

Yet we confess that this image is scarred and defaced. This is our human condition, and it is the present moment. The people called Methodist see this as an altar call to serve the present age. And this service takes the form of healing, the healing we need, and the healing we can offer to each other.

Study Questions

1. What grief and loss has your church experienced?

2. Have you been provoked by a difference of opinion in the church, the community, or the country? What would "provoke you to love"?

3. What personal gifts do you bring for loving God and loving neighbors in reconstructing your church and your community?

Four

Unrelenting Grace and the Healing of Our Bodies (Churches)

Healing: The Forgotten Ministry of Jesus

Early in ministry, shortly after graduation, I was serving a charge of four churches. Two churches were nearly in sight of each other and had separated during the Civil War. One had been a Southern church, one a Northern church. One was named "New Home" and was literally the "new home" of the other one. Methodists have separated before. It is in our DNA. I was sent to be the shepherd to the saints in both houses of worship.

On Sunday mornings, I was usually the first person to arrive in the church parking lot at New Home. I needed time to get things ready. One morning, a car was already in the parking lot, and I could see that a man was seated in it. It was early, I thought. I went inside to prepare and began to meet folks who streamed in, the ushers, the organist. People came in, sat in the pews, and I noticed the man from the car found a side pew near the front. I realized that I had met him. His name was Marvin, and I would see him from time to time at the fish camp, which was one of the two restaurants in town.

The congregation gathered, and the organist began. The chimes of the hour rang. I could hear people whispering, "There's Marvin." "Marvin is here." "Marvin is over there." One could hear people saying his name!

When the service ended, I shook Marvin's hand and asked if I could call him. He said yes, so I made a mental note to call him that afternoon. No one shows up that early for church without a reason.

I called him and we arranged that I would visit with him and his wife the next evening. I went to his house, and after some small talk he said, "I was listening to a preacher on the radio"—and I thought, this can't be a good thing—"and the preacher said, 'if anyone is sick, call the elders of the church, and they will pray for you and you will be anointed with oil.'"

Then he looked at me and asked, "Are you the kind of preacher who anoints people with oil?" And then, more quietly, "Would you do that for me?"

He went on to say that he was sick. We moved to some other small talk—maybe we needed to lessen the intensity—and then I prayed and asked if I could come back the next night. He said that would be fine.

I was around twenty-five years old, so the next morning I called a couple of older ministers, just to ask if they had done something like this anointing. They both said yes, you can do this. I read James 5, and then I read it a second time and a third. I imagined being there with Marvin. Early in the afternoon I called our lay leader, Dale, and asked if he would go with me. He said he would, although I suspect he had never seen something like this in the job description of a lay leader.

We arrived at Marvin's home. We made some small talk. When I sensed the right moment, I asked if we could read the scripture and anoint Marvin. He was ready. I read James 5:13-20 and allowed some time for silence. Then I asked Marvin if there was anything he would like to confess. After an extended time of silence, Marvin broke the silence: He was a big man, a construction worker, and I have never heard a groan as loud from a person. He began to cry and confessed—to his wife, to me—about his son, with whom he was estranged. They had once worked together in construction but were now competitors. He confessed his lack of love.

After it was quiet again, I assured him that we were all sinners, that we all fall short of the glory of God. When we stood, I moved toward him and touched the oil and made the sign of the cross on his forehead. I announced that he had been healed, in the name of the Father, the Son, and the Holy Spirit.

After a few minutes we walked out into the night. On the ride back to the parsonage, where Dale left his car, he and I didn't say a word to each other. We had been on holy ground.

Much more recently, I was asked to preach in a congregation on a Sunday morning. As the date approached, the staff-parish relations committee asked if I could meet with them. There was some conflict in this church, and the pastor would be transitioning, which was already a mutual agreement. Over lunch they shared with me some data from their church, some present challenges, and then the very articulate chair said, "We need a pastor who will return the church to its former glory."

I allowed for a brief silence, and then I responded. "I want to honor the work that went into what you have just shared. And I want to lay alongside of it a question. Is it possible that what you are experiencing right now in this church—what you see as a challenge—is it possible that it has nothing to do with your pastor? Could it be something else? I am not saying I know what that is, but could it be something else? And what could that be?"

There was a longer silence. Then someone spoke up. "We are divided. I can't remember a time in my life when we were more divided. It is everywhere: in the family, in my neighborhood, in the city, in my Sunday school class, in this church, in our nation, in the denomination. That is what it is."

We share a common need for healing in body and spirit.

Sometime after this meeting I was walking through a store. I stepped in some water, fell, and fractured my humerus (shoulder). It was painful, even traumatic. This set me on a journey with X-ray technicians, nurses, physical therapists, physician assistants, and a surgeon. I was often in pain. And I would find myself saying a simple prayer to God: "Let the person I meet today be a healing person."

If you are in ministry or if you are in the church, right now, you are in touch with a great deal of pain. Your diagnostic work is to discover where the pain is most acute. Could that healing person be you?

Marvin and his wife came to church regularly. People began to see them as family and not as a curious presence. I would often see Marvin and his son together at the fish camp. You could say that they experienced a reconciliation. His cancer also progressed, and then, a few months later, Marvin went into hospice. The story I shared here is one he asked me to tell at his memorial service.

The ultimate healing is in the resurrection. We read in James 5:15: "Prayer that comes from faith will heal the sick, for the Lord will restore them to health. And if they have sinned, they will be forgiven." Many of us prayed for the healing of loved ones who are no longer with us in the body.

We believe that the ultimate healing is in the resurrection. Return to the vision around the throne in Revelation 21:3-5: "God himself will be with them as their God. He will wipe away every tear from their eyes. Death will be no more. There will be no mourning, crying, or pain anymore, for the former things have passed away." Then the one seated on the throne said, "Look! I'm making all things new." Not everything that is broken in this life will be made whole in this life. The ultimate healing is in the resurrection.

The ministry of healing, so prominent in the life of Jesus, does not end with his earthly ministry. We, his followers, are sent out into the world to be healers, sometimes (in the language of Henri Nouwen) as wounded healers. We read in Luke 9:2, "He sent them out to proclaim God's kingdom and to heal the sick." From the Jewish Mishnah (a first-century oral commentary on Torah instruction) is the phrase *tikkun olam*, which means "to repair the world." Some deeds, some actions are not required by the law, but they should be done anyway, "for the sake of the repair of the world." For you and me, the teaching is compelling: we may not have an obligation or a duty, but there is some action laid upon us that we can do to repair a relationship, to heal a division, to bring about reconciliation.

In a season of disagreements and disaffiliations, misinformation and inequalities, privilege and desperation, pandemic and estrangement, we pray for healing persons to cross our paths. With vulnerability, we pray for the healing that we ourselves need, and for the courage ourselves to be healing persons and a healing church, in a time with so much trauma and disrepair.

Healing and the Integrity of the Body

The United Methodist Church needs healing. Many have experienced harm or even trauma. Relationships are fractured. Some members lost churches to whom they were devoted for a lifetime. Local churches and even communities are weakened. We need healing.

The good news is that we place our ultimate faith and hope in the One who has the power to heal us. God's healing is the pathway to the re-membering of our bodies: our friendships, our churches, our communities.

On one occasion, Jesus enters the synagogue on the Sabbath, and he teaches. The place is important, and the day is important. He is in God's place. This is God's time. Capernaum was a small village in the Galilee; the ruins of the synagogue still stand today. Jesus as the Messiah had been foretold by John in the desert. Jesus had been baptized in the Jordan River. Jesus had been tempted, and he withstood the trials of the wilderness. Now he announces the coming of God's kingdom; he calls the first disciples.

Jesus is in the synagogue teaching, and Mark tells us that he is "teaching them with authority," not like the legal experts (Mark 1:22).

Authority is an important word. It signifies the coming together of the roles we have in life—in our family, in our workplace, in the church—into the person that we are. It is also about the coming together of our words and our actions. Authority is about *integrity*. The legal experts (scribes) had the role of teaching about the Torah (the law), but they lost touch with the real meaning of the instruction. The legal experts knew the words and the acts of piety, but their actions did not embody those words. This disconnection can easily happen. I might know the words of the scriptures, even the original languages in which they were written, but that doesn't mean I'm ready to listen to the instructions or act on them. It isn't accidental in Luke 15 that a legal expert passes by the man who fell among thieves in Jesus's telling of the parable of the good Samaritan.

Sometimes our actions don't embody our words. One of the most memorable sermons in my life was a children's sermon. The minister gathered a group of children together, and she spoke like this: "Children, I have made an important decision. I saw the doctor this week, and I need to do something about my health. So I'm going on a diet." Here she opens a big candy bar, takes a huge bite, and begins to chew. She talks while she's eating. "If I don't change my way of eating, I'm going to be in trouble." She takes another big bite. Then she says, "I'm going to limit my eating to fruits and vegetables, mostly, a little meat, and no sweets." Then another big bite!

The children's eyes are getting bigger at this point. She goes on: "I also need to tell you that I'm growing stronger as a Christian too. This week I've been reading in the Bible about sharing, and I think sharing is what God wants all of us to do." She takes another big bite and finishes that candy bar. Then she opens another one, holds it there for a moment, and continues. "Sharing is what life is all about" (then she takes another big bite while talking), "sharing what we have with others. Don't you think sharing is important?" By now the kids are almost jumping off the floor in protest!

"You're not sharing," a little girl said to her. Of course, she was right! In her own way the child was saying, your teaching has no authority.

Authority doesn't come from credentials, positions, or even achievements. Jesus had no formal education, no recognized title, nothing to claim for himself in the way of authority, except for one thing: his relationship with God. His authority came from God, and it was an authority that he used very sparingly: he came not to be served but to serve, and to give his life as a reconciling mediator for many.

In the Capernaum synagogue, on the Sabbath, Jesus meets a man with an evil spirit (Mark 1:21-27). It is not always true that the Holy Spirit is in the church and the evil spirit is in the world. Sometimes the foul spirit is in the church and the Holy Spirit is at work in the world. Jesus encounters the evil spirit in the form of a man who says to him, "What have you to do with us, Jesus of Nazareth?

Have you come to destroy us? . . . You are the holy one from God" (v. 24).

At our best, within our churches and beyond them, we live in the tension between foul spirits and the Holy Spirit.

The evil spirit takes; the Holy Spirit gives.

The evil spirit divides; the Holy Spirit unifies.

The evil spirit confuses; the Holy Spirit reveals.

The evil spirit discourages; the Holy Spirit encourages.

The evil spirit recognizes that Jesus comes in the power of the Holy Spirit. Jesus says to the evil spirit, "Silence! . . . Come out" (v. 25). At the beginning of the Gospel, there is a recognition and naming of evil in the world. Jesus doesn't look away. Jesus doesn't avoid the foul spirit. Jesus says, "Silence! Come out."

How might the church of Jesus say, "Silence! Come out" when we encounter the foul spirits of our time?

We have not always done well at recognizing our foul spirits, and this, in part, is why the church does not generally have great authority in our culture. We have not always recognized the unclean spirits or called them to come out and be silent. At times we have supported unjust laws and inhumane systems. At times we have been silent, or we have looked the other way as real suffering takes place. Our integrity is in question, whether the unclean or foul spirit has been racism, genocide, discrimination against queer persons, sexual trafficking of children or adults, destruction of the environment, or poisonous greed.

The church has not spoken to the foul spirit and said, "Silence! Come out." We are not talking about being politically expedient, politically correct, or politically partisan. We are conferring about the integrity of the gospel.

Where Jesus is, people of all identities are healed. Where Jesus is, relationships are restored. Where Jesus is, life flourishes. Where Jesus is, there is wholeness. Where Jesus is, there is integrity. The church finds itself in a culture of foul spirits, and sometimes the church itself is fully immersed in that culture.

Jesus speaks to the man with an evil spirit and says, "Come out." And the foul spirit comes out, "convulsing him," Mark says, "with a loud voice" (v. 26 NRSVue). This is the trauma of being healed. This is the difficult process of being purged. It's like we have been dragged out of the water, and we are struggling to breathe. Our lungs have been polluted, and the evil spirit/breath within us has filled us to the degree that it must come out, and it is painful.

Salvation is never easy. Something dies. The old passes away. Paul writes to the church in Corinth, "new things have arrived" (2 Corinthians 5:17). Salvation involves confession and a change of hearts and lives. The evil spirit was right; Jesus came to destroy something. But it was more in the spirit of a surgeon who removes something, a tumor, so that the patient might live.

Everything opposed to God is destroyed in us. Paul, writing to the Galatians (5:19-23), describes this well as actions produced by our selfish motives: "sexual immorality, moral corruption, doing whatever feels good, idolatry, drug use and casting spells, hate, fighting, obsession, losing your temper, competitive opposition, conflict, selfishness, group rivalry, jealousy, drunkenness, partying, and other things like that" (5:19-21). If we are honest, we see these mindsets and behaviors in ourselves, and we struggle to detach from them.

In contrast to our selfish desires—we might also call them the evil spirits—there is the fruit of the Spirit: "Love, joy, peace, patience, kindness, goodness, faithfulness, gentleness, and self-control" (5:22-23).

In the synagogue in Capernaum, on the Sabbath, there ensued a struggle between the foul spirit and the Holy Spirit in the life of Jesus. The good news is that the power of God in Jesus Christ is always greater than the evil powers of this world. And yet the great battle, good over evil, fruit of the Spirit over selfish desire, often takes place in small ways and in hidden places. We choose not to retaliate; we decide not to say something that is hurtful; we forgive; we speak the truth in love; we move on; we let something go; we extend compassion.

The people are amazed at what Jesus has done, and word gets out. He teaches with authority. What if a different word got out about United Methodists? What if we spoke with the voice of Jesus in calling out the evil spirits of our time? And what if we had the humility to recognize the evil spirits that live within us?

United Methodists have lived through disease and trauma. Some of our wounds are self-inflicted. We do violence to each other. And we live in a world whose cynicism yearns for transparency, a world that is jaded by religious pretense and yet longs for authenticity, a world damaged by fractured relationships and one that now searches for reconciliation. This is not a time for positive thinking, avoidance, or living in denial. In the imagery of the Apostle Paul, this is a time to name "the forces of cosmic darkness, and spiritual powers of evil" (Ephesians 6:12).

This is a moment to acknowledge that we are, all of us, the man with the foul spirit. We are all asking, "If the gospel has really penetrated our hearts and minds, Jesus, what do you want to do with us?" And we must all confess with him, "I know who you are, Jesus: You have come to destroy us!"

Only when we ask that question—"Jesus, what do you want to do with us?"—and only when we make that confession—"I know who you are, Jesus: You have come to destroy us"—only then will we know that he is "The Holy One of God"; only then will the healing begin. Only then will we know the purging that is part of our sanctification in this season. Then will we contribute to the integrity of the body that is incorporated as The United Methodist Church.

Sustain the Basic Practices

As we move from disruptions and trauma into the future, we are called to take the next faithful steps through many unknowns. What will our experience of church and community become? What shape will our discipleship take? How will we find meaning and purpose in sharing our gifts? Some of us will take all that we have experienced—some of which has shaken or disoriented us in some way—to make a fresh beginning. How can we do the work of Jesus in the way of Jesus?

Remember three simple practices to revise or improve for your context.

Welcome Unconditionally

Our culture, for better or worse, has a default way of labeling us, according to who we appear to be externally, or where our political sympathies lie, or by the accents that carry the words that we speak. We label each other, we form judgments, we imagine that we might have something in common with this person, or we assume that we do not.

In the ministry of the church of Jesus Christ, shared by laity and clergy, we are called to welcome unconditionally. We see this hospitality pattern in the life of Jesus himself. He ate with sinners. He crossed ethnic boundaries. He touched the unclean. Jesus had the inner mark of holiness and the outer mark of compassion. We are called to represent Jesus, the good shepherd.

Our lives now are not our own. We represent Jesus, the good news of Jesus, the unconditional love of God. "While we were still weak, at the right moment, Christ died for ungodly people. . . . While we were still sinners, Christ died for us," the Apostle Paul wrote (Romans 5:6, 8). While the prodigal was at a distance, the father ran and embraced him (Luke 15).

A local pastor I knew served a small town where many worked in nearby factories. The pastor learned of a member in one of the active families who was serving time for murder and was on death row. The pastor drove a hundred miles each way every Saturday to visit with the young man. He did this for two years. The church supported this because he was being a pastor, a shepherd to the family.

And then events took a strange turn. Another inmate in the prison was overheard saying that he had, in fact, committed the murder. Soon the church member was released. He returned home. The congregation threw a great banquet; the son had returned! It was a celebration.

The story didn't end there. The man who confessed the murder contacted that same pastor and asked if he would visit him. As one called to be a shepherd, he began to do just that. Every Saturday the pastor would drive one hundred miles each way to visit the inmate. He learned along the way that the church didn't support this so much. But he had a calling to welcome unconditionally.

He and the man in prison formed a bond. And in time the inmate asked him, "Would you be present at my execution?" And then, "Would you officiate at my graveside service?" That pastor would indeed be present at his execution and officiate at his burial.

There is power in welcoming people unconditionally. This power is embedded in every page of the Gospels, in the rhythm of Jesus's very life, death, and resurrection.

Meetings of the Council of Bishops often begin with a memorial service for bishops and spouses who died that year. On one evening, those remembered were Julia Wilke, co-author of the *DISCIPLE Bible Study*; Eunice Mathews, widow of Bishop James Mathews and daughter of E. Stanley Jones; and retired bishop Rueben Job, former world editor of the Upper Room, author of *A Guide to Prayer for Ministers and Servants* and *Three Simple Rules*. Bruce Ough, now a retired bishop for the Dakotas and Minnesota, offered a remembrance. Bruce mentioned a question he asked Rueben Job near the end of his life. "What are you learning spiritually? What is the Lord teaching you?"

Rueben Job responded, "Everyone is God's beloved child. God doesn't make the distinctions that we make."

Welcome unconditionally. Many scholars believe the purpose of John 21, which was attached to the Gospel later, was to reintegrate Peter into the life of the community, to restore him. Peter had denied Jesus three times and abandoned him. Now he is asked, three times, "Do you love me?" And Jesus says, "Feed my sheep. Follow me."

One of our important radical practices in the next season is to reintegrate those who have become separated from the community back into the fellowship.

Walk Together

A second practice: walk together. For a variety of reasons, we are tempted at times to go through this life alone. This may be related to the myth of the heroic solo leader, or the egoism of self-reliance, or sometimes it may just seem to be the path of least resistance. Other people are too complicated. I will do it myself!

But be encouraged to walk together. A mural is painted on the wall of the airport in Johannesburg, South Africa, including the words:

> If you want to go fast, walk alone.
> If you want to go far, walk together.

In the shared ministry of Jesus, you will want to walk together. We have a word for this: the *connection*. The connection has a purpose, to help us grow spiritually and to love our neighbor. This is the practical heart of Methodism. Connection is our way of fulfilling the great commandment of Jesus (Matthew 22) on which hangs all the Law and the Prophets.

Currently, the connection is *strained*. The connection itself is contested. And now it is fractured. The loss of connection is about loss of friendship and vocation and identity.

It calls into question who we have been and are and want to be with others.

But those structural flaws are not the end of the connection, because the connection is rooted in the works of piety and the works of mercy, the practices through which we are accountable to each other. This happens more easily in small circles of trust and is less likely in very large groups (such as political conferences).

Works of piety and mercy are a part of my own life. Works of piety include reading the New Testament and the Psalms and *The Imitation of Christ*. Other pious behavior includes prayer, especially intercession, and corporate worship, receiving Holy Communion as often as possible.

Works of mercy for me include encouragement of others, a disciplined lifestyle and healing habits, my roles as husband and father and grandparent, becoming more serious about charitable giving, figuring out how mercy blends into justice, and engaging in politics in appropriate (principled and non-partisan) ways.

Love of neighbor isn't easy because the neighbor has increasingly become a stranger. Strangers are more pervasive when we are more siloed and even tribal. For a rich description of public, familiar, and intimate strangers, see Gregory Ellison's *Fearless Dialogues*.

How can strangers become neighbors? In the parable of the good Samaritan (Luke 10), the question is asked of Jesus, "Who is my neighbor?"

When Wesley says that there is no holiness but social holiness, he is saying there is no way to fulfill the great commandment apart from connection. We can't be disciples apart from connection. And we can't transform the world apart from being disciples. Connection is in service of our way of making disciples of Jesus Christ for the transformation of the world.

Whenever there is connection, there is hope. When there is no connection, we experience less *happiness* and *holiness*, words that were synonyms for Wesley.

Holy living is a set of practices that puts us in a place to mature. The presence of other faithful people helps us to practice our faith. This looks like a mature spirituality and a corresponding compassion. We can't love God, whom we have never seen, if we don't love our neighbor, whom we have seen.

We need a new canon of teaching rooted in Matthew 22 and Galatians 5 and Luke 10. The latter includes both the great commandment and parable of the good Samaritan. The neighbor question is sometimes harder for us. It is, of course, a test of our salvation. These core passages of scripture can shape the way we see, honor, and love our neighbors.

Our happiness and holiness are based in our neighbor's well-being, that is, being surrounded by more neighbors than strangers. So how do strangers become neighbors? How does the familiar become intimate?

- Curiosity, conversation, and risk.
- Seeing others without labels and imagining them to be more mysterious and complex than we had first thought.
- Assuming the best about them.
- Meals, the reciprocity of giving and receiving, knowing that this takes time and patience.
- Being willing to change our minds about others and giving them second chances. Many of us are in the church because we were given some kind of second chance.

Jesus sees us more as neighbors than strangers. Indeed, he calls us his friends (John 15:15).

Connection will require courage from those of us in leadership. It takes courage to see the stranger who is near to us as a neighbor we are called to love. It takes courage to grow the center and risk not being in full agreement with those on the convictional edges. It takes energy to keep people in connection with each other so they will grow into the maturity of their callings as disciples, as leaders.

It takes courage to stay at a very contentious table. It would be easier to take a last sip of tea, push back our chair, and walk away to the certainty of the convictional ledge. As if we jump into something there. Maybe something disastrous.

It takes courage to sing with Al Green, "Let's Stay Together." It takes courage and creativity to grow the center, to find some new form of unity. The center is the most inclusive space because it wants to keep as many as possible in connection.

The connection is the heart of Methodism. It is the heart of Jesus. It bears the weight of everything. Are we willing to bear this weight with each other and for the sake of the church we love? Do we understand that the world is watching to see if we will walk together?

Worship Constantly

A third practice: worship God.

"My sheep listen to my voice. I know them and they follow me" (John 10:27). How do we hear the voice of Jesus the Good Shepherd? We immerse ourselves in the scriptures and we pray them.

Along the way, many of us learned to deconstruct and dissect the scriptures, and then stopped before letting the scripture become words that make us whole, heal us, save us, and bring us into alignment with the One who creates us, who calls us and claims us. As these words make us whole, they have the capacity to speak through us, when we let our lives speak.

Worship constantly. Pray without ceasing. Let the word of Christ dwell in you richly. Sing psalms and hymns and spiritual songs.

Years ago, I heard an ordination sermon given by a bishop who made a bold assertion, and one that seemed at the time to be fairly unscientific! "If you are not reading scripture and praying every day, you will not be in the ministry in seven years." Years later, I know that bishop was onto something for each of us, lay or clergy.

We build up capital early in the spiritual life: by being mentored by teachers, by sermons that inspire us, by friends and supporters who encourage us. This energy is like capital that builds up, and it is there to use. Then we draw it down and spend it down, and we wake up one day running on empty!

In this moment we are in spiritual danger. Living becomes about ego, or performance, or people-pleasing. We can no longer hear the voice. It has become faint, drowned out by the noise of the culture, the marketplace, the media, and the politicians.

Then we see the church differently. Dietrich Bonhoeffer spoke of the shattering of our "wish dream" of community (*Life Together*, p. 30). All people, we included, are broken, imperfect, and sinful. And yet, in the mystery of providence, Jesus chooses us, chooses you to constitute his body or lead his flock.

How do we sustain this? How do we do the work of Jesus in the way of Jesus? To worship constantly is to be driven back to the admonition of the Apostle Paul: "Don't be conformed to the patterns of this world but be transformed by the renewing of your minds" (Romans 12:2).

To worship constantly is to know that we don't do this by our own strength; none of us. To worship constantly is to return to the streams of renewal, to the holy book, to the holy places, to the holy people.

We are called to leadership in this time, which is an adventure amid a turbulent and chaotic season. Something needs to happen. Something needs to change. Someone is searching for us, the lost sheep. Someone is willing to give us all that we need, which is the grace of bread and wine. Someone is willing to lead us, and to transform our leadership to the degree that we are willing to be led. As Lesslie Newbigin wrote in his commentary on John 21, *The Light Has Come*, before we are shepherds or fishers of men and women, we are first disciples.

"My sheep hear my voice," Jesus says, "and I know them, and they follow me." How do we follow Jesus? We:

> Welcome unconditionally.
> Walk together.
> Worship constantly.

This is our calling, together. If we commit ourselves to these spiritual practices, if we are faithful, our life together will be fruitful. And where there is faithfulness and fruitfulness, there is unity.

A Prayer for Sending Forth

We are formed by the prayers we offer—to God, for each other, and for the world. The Collect for Purity can be traced to the tenth century. It was in the Prayer Book that shaped the Wesleys, and it is found in our *United Methodist Hymnal.* It is a prayer that John Wesley used at the conclusion of his *A Plain Account of Christian Perfection.*

May the words of this common prayer sustain us, for the living of these days.

> Almighty God,
>
> to you all hearts are opened, all desires known,
>
> and from you no secrets are hidden.
>
> Cleanse the thoughts of our hearts
>
> by the inspiration of your Holy Spirit,
>
> that we may perfectly love you,
>
> and worthily magnify your holy name,
>
> through Christ our Lord.
>
> Amen.
>
> (A Service of Word and Table I, *UM Hymnal,* p. 6)

Study Questions

1. Describe where you see division in your extended family, in your neighborhood, in your town or city, in your Sunday school class, in your church, in the nation, and in the denomination.

2. Healing is often expressed through a story. Can you tell a story about healing?

3. What foul spirit needs to come out of your church?

4. What acts of mercy do you practice consistently? What acts of piety sustain your spirit?

5. Who in your church nurtures healing? Who in your church models constant worship? What are instances when you've seen your congregation work as a whole to promote healing?

Sources

Adichie, Chimamanda. "The Danger of a Single Story," October 7, 2009. https://www.ted.com/talks/chimamanda_ngozi
_adichie_the_danger_of_a_single_story.

Arbinger Institute, The. *The Anatomy of Peace: Resolving the Heart of Conflict*, 4th ed. Oakland, CA: Berrett-Koehler Publishers, 2022.

Bonhoeffer, Dietrich. *Life Together*. San Francisco: Harper and Row, 1954.

Carter, Kenneth H. Jr. "Patience, Peace, and the Promise of God: A Christmas Message from Bishop Carter." December 20, 2022. https://www.wnccumc.org/newsdetail/patience-peace
-and-the-promise-of-god-a-christmas-message-from-bishop
-carter-17188854.

Cobb, Jelani. "Inside the Trial of Dylann Roof." *The New Yorker*, February 6, 2017.

Ellison, Gregory. *Fearless Dialogues*. Louisville: Westminster John Knox, 2017.

Hays, Richard. "The Word of Reconciliation." *Faith and Leadership*, July 19, 2010.

Job, Rueben. *A Wesleyan Spiritual Reader.* Nashville: Abingdon, 1998.

Langford, Thomas. *Practical Divinity: Theology in the Wesleyan Tradition*, rev. ed., vol. 1. Nashville: Abingdon, 1998.

Marshall, Jane. "What Gift Can We Bring." In *The United Methodist Hymnal*, no. 87. Nashville: The United Methodist Publishing House, 1989.

Newbigin, Lesslie. *The Light Has Come: An Exposition of the Fourth Gospel.* United Kingdom: W. B. Eerdmans, 1982.

Nouwen, Henri J. M. "A Spirituality of Waiting," audio. Notre Dame, IN: Ave Maria Press, 2014. https://www.avemariapress.com/products/a-spirituality-of-waiting-mp3.

Outler, Albert C., and Richard P. Heitzenrater, eds. *John Wesley's Sermons.* Nashville: Abingdon Press, 1991.

Rutledge, Fleming. "Generous Orthodoxy: A Statement of Purpose." https://generousorthodoxy.org/ (accessed March 21, 2023).

Sacks, Jonathan. *Not in God's Name.* New York: Schocken, 2015.

———. "Righteousness Is Not Leadership." *Covenant and Conversation*, October 5, 2013. https://www.rabbisacks.org/app/uploads/2013/09/CC-5774-Noah-Righteousness-is-not-Leadership.pdf.

United Methodist Bishops. "A Narrative for the Continuing United Methodist Church," November 4, 2021. https://www.unitedmethodistbishops.org/files/websites/www/a+narrative+for+the+continuing+united+methodist+church...._.pdf.

United Methodist Book of Discipline, The. Nashville: The United Methodist Publishing House, 2016.

United Methodist Hymnal, The. Nashville: The United Methodist Publishing House, 1989.

CPSIA information can be obtained
at www.ICGtesting.com
Printed in the USA
LVHW021311040423
743420LV00002B/3